The Paper Bead

Simple DIY Paper Beads

© 2020 All rights reserved

TABLE OF CONTENT

HISTORY OF PAPER BEAD MAKING:	3
29 TYPES OF PAPER FOR MAKING PAPER BEADS	5
HOW TO MAKE PAPER BEADS	20
THREE POPULAR TYPE OF PAPER BEADS	31
SEALING PAPER BEADS - WHICH METHOD IS BEST?	34

History of Paper Bead Making:

Making paper beads is a traditional craft that goes back, in England at least, as far as the Victorian age. Young ladies would gather socially in their dining rooms, whilst making handmade paper beads from scraps of wallpaper rolled on knitting needles. They would then polish the beads with bees wax and string them on to long pieces of yarn. They would then be used to make door curtains to divide rooms.

This practice was then revived in the 1920s and 30s for paper bead jewellery making.

More recently artist made paper beads have been made in cooperatives as part of development projects in countries such as Uganda. This sees a move away from charitable aid towards business enterprises that provide sustainable income and development opportunities. The techniques used for African paper beads remains largely the same as used in Victorian times, but with scrap paper from printing companies and paper recycling markets, rather than wallpaper samples. The most notable enterprise of this nature is a Scottish based company called Mzuribeads who market and sell ethical Ugandan paper beads, as well as cow horn beads, barkcloth beads, banana leaf beads and lampwork beads made from recycled glass.

29 Types of Paper for Making Paper Beads

One of the best things about making jewelry with rolled paper beads is the huge number of sources to get your paper. Almost any type of paper that is flexible enough to roll into a cylinder is can be used for making paper beads. Once you start looking around, you'll notice sources for paper beads everywhere! Experimenting with different types, weights, colors, and thicknesses of paper is a great way to expand your creativity.

Types of Paper for Making Beads

1. **Magazines** – Magazine paper usually has shiny colors from all the photos. It usually has a glossy coating on it that is a little bit more water resistant than regular copier paper. Because the paper is usually very thin and lightweight, it requires longer strips to get a thicker diameter bead.

2. **Newspapers** – Newspapers often have a lot of text and be fun for getting beads that have words on them.

3. **Notebooks** – Blank or used. This can be interesting for getting beads with handwritten text on them.

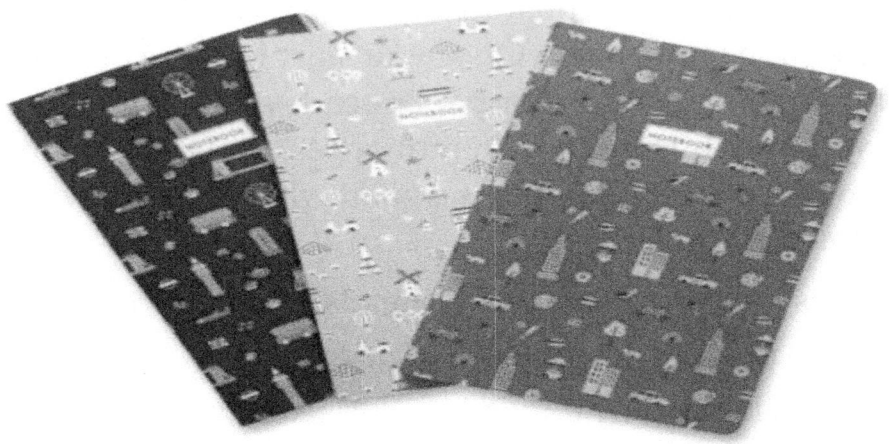

4. **Wrapping Paper** – When the birthday party is done or the holidays or over, this is a great way to get brightly colored beads. I find it a little harder to use because some inexpensive wrapping paper is so thin and sometimes the colors crack or come off if it gets too wet when you are making the bead. You'll want to seal these to protect them.

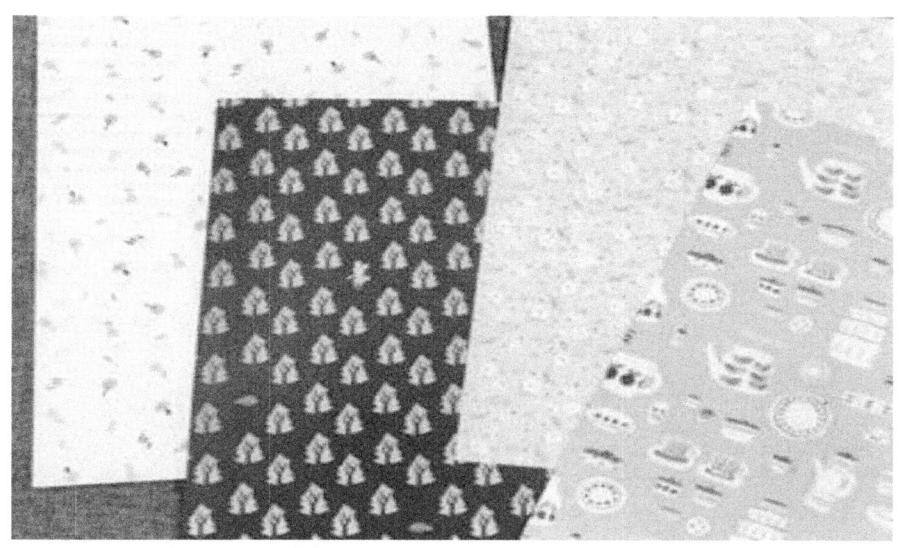

5. **Printer/Copier Paper** – I like using this type of paper because it is pretty sturdy. However, because it's not shiny, if you want glossy beads, you'll need to varnish it or coat is with something that will add gloss after you make your beads.

6. **Scrapbooking paper** – Scrapbooking paper comes in lots of different patterns and colors and can make really interesting beads. There is even glitter scrapbook paper that can make really exciting looking beads for jewelry. Make sure you are using the thin paper and not cardstock. Cardstock scrapbooking paper is too thick and won't roll well.

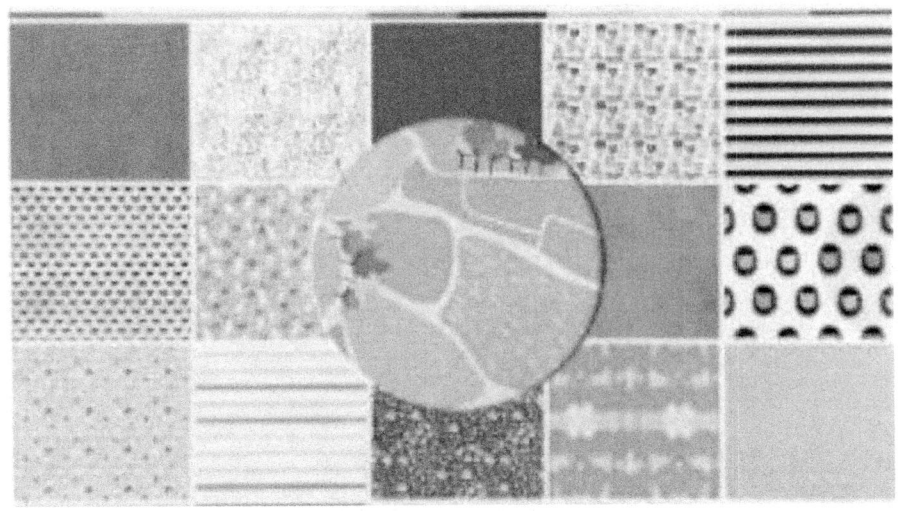

7. **Tissue Paper** – Tissue paper is too thin to use on its own to make paper beads. However, if you combine it with a sturdier paper or make layered tissue paper before you use it for beads, it can make gorgeous paper.

8. **Paper Grocery Bags** – Bags that you bring home from the grocery store can make great sturdy beads that have a very natural look to them.

9. **Old books** – Old books (especially kids books) are a wonderful source for beads with text or interesting colors on them.

10. **Origami paper** – I've seen some absolutely gorgeous beads done with origami paper. Rather than making an oval bead, you may want to consider making a cylinder bead with origami paper so that you can see more of the design.

11. **Junk Mail** – One of my favorite sources for paper beads. It is a free and never-ending source of paper.

12. **Tracing paper** – If thin and flexible enough, this can make an interesting translucent bead.

13. **Catalogs** – Catalogs get out of date quickly, but can make wonderful beads. The paper is often shiny and coated like the magazines.

14. **Old Schoolwork** – Rather than throwing last year's schoolwork papers away, roll some of them into beads.

15. **Flyers** – Flyers for old events are not needed anymore. Turn them into jewelry by making them into beads.

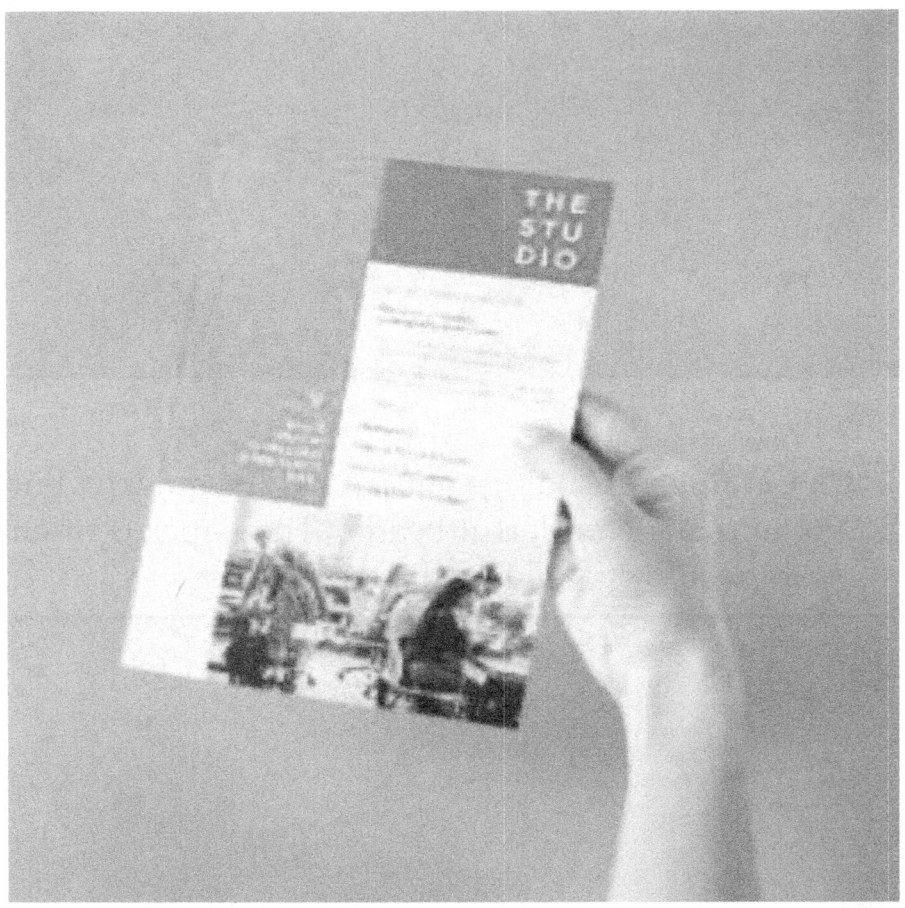

16. **Posters** – Old unwanted posters can make great beads. They are usually heavyweight paper and have lots of colors.

17. **Wallpaper** – I've never tried wallpaper, but I have heard of it being used. The patterns would be great for making pretty beads. Supposedly Victorian women used wallpaper to make beads.

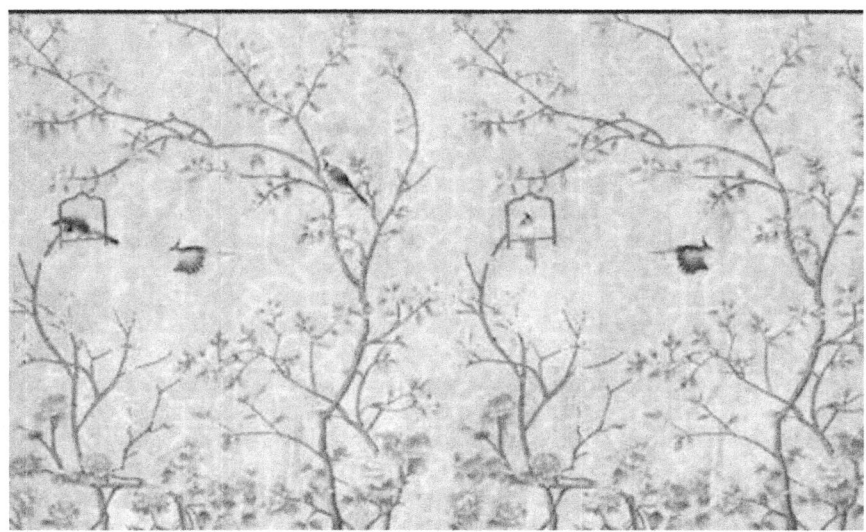

18. **Handmade Paper** – Handmade paper has an interesting rough texture and can make beautiful beads. (Make sure that it is flexible enough to roll.)

19. **Dust Jackets** – These usually fall off of books, and if you're the type of get rid of them, consider using them for paper beads. They are very study and often shiny and colorful and make great beads.

20. **Used Coloring Books** – If your child has gotten tired of the book, this would be a great way to recycle it.

21. **Phonebooks** – Lots and lots of paper these!

22. **Brown Paper Lunch Bags** – If the paper is still clean, recycle them into beads.

23. **Paper Towels** – I'm planning on trying this, but I bet this makes a really interesting textured bead. However, since it is so absorbent, I would guess you would have to seal it pretty well if you want to use it in jewelry.

24. **Ultrafine Grit Sandpaper** – Again, never tried this, but this could be an interesting experiment!

25. **Movie Tickets** – These might be a little thick, but they would make an interesting commemorative bead.

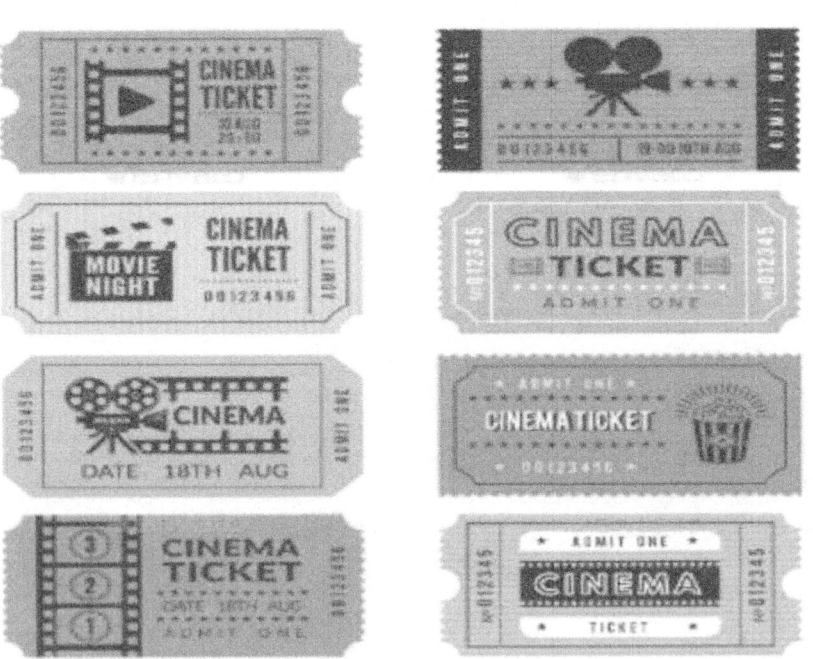

26. **Maps** – Lots of cool text for the beads.

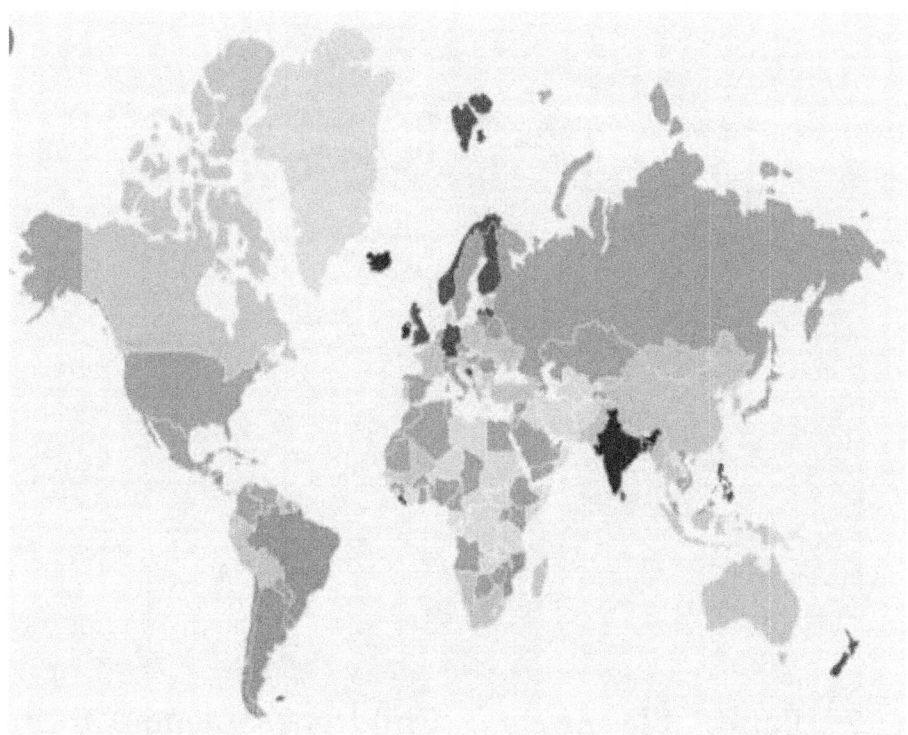

27. **Napkins** – Probably would have the same issue as the paper towels, but might be worth trying.

28. **Old Calendars** – Colorful photos. Flexible, sturdy, coated pages. These would be great for beads.

29. **Paper Placemats** – Children's menus from restaurants.

Warning:

- Paper Bead Care – having been varnished paper beads will survive a rain shower but they don't like to go swimming or to do the washing up!
- Paper beading is highly addictive!

How To Make Paper Beads

1. Tools And Materials:

- **Paper**
- **Pencil** – for marking up the paper.

- **Ruler** – for measuring up.

- **Craft Knife, Rotary Cutter or Scissors** – for cutting out. If you are using scissors you should use the longest pair available so as to reduce the number of cuts required along each length.

- **Straight Edge** – for cutting against.

- **Self Healing Cutting Mat** – for cutting on.

- **Metal Skewer or Thin Wooden Dowel** – for rolling paper against. Commercially made paper bead rollers are also available.

- **Soft Paint Brush** – for applying glue to the paper.

- **Glue** – for securing your rolled beads. Undiluted PVA is perfect but there are many other alternatives including glue sticks.

- **Wooden Cocktail Sticks** – for holding your rolled beads when drying or when varnishing.

- **Soft Paint Brush** – for applying varnish. A quality brush is preferable at this point as it is less likely to leave bristles on the surface of your beads

- **Varnish** – for waterproofing your rolled beads. Quick drying marine varnish is perfect and is usually touch dry within 1 hour and ready for a second coat in 4 hours. Experiment with gloss, satin, matt, and antique coloured varnishes for different finishes.

- **Oasis Florist Block, Polystyrene Block, or similar** – for securing the beads whilst varnishing and drying. Push a cocktail stick holding an individual bead securely into the block.

2. Basic Paper Bead Making Tutorial:

Step 1. Place your paper face down on your work surface so that the side facing you is not the side that will form the outside of the bead

Step 2. With a sharp pencil mark up the reverse side of your paper sample by marking-up one short edge of your paper with divisions spaced 30mm apart. On the opposite short edge of your paper make a mark 15mm in from the edge and then continue with divisions 30mm apart. In this way you should have the makings of a long isosceles triangle when you join two adjacent marks on the first edge, points A and B, with the central mark on the opposing edge, point

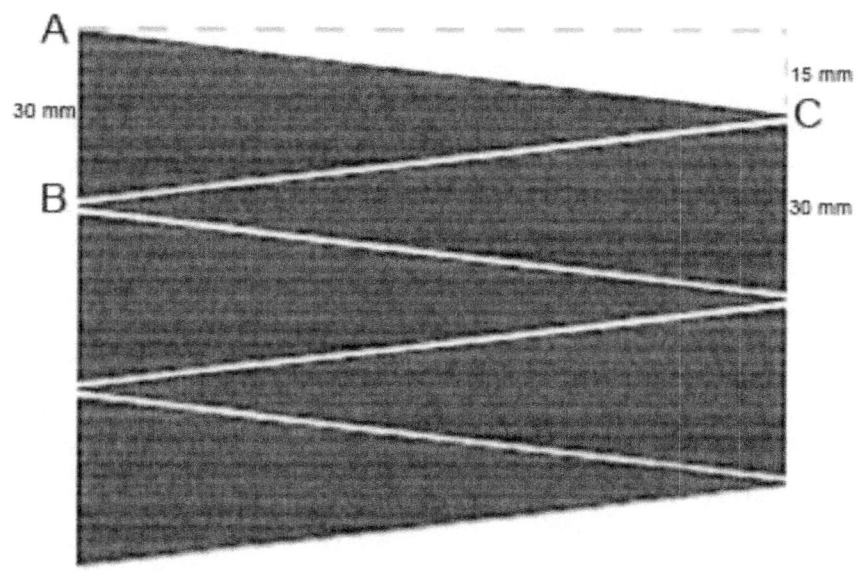

Step 3. Continue marking up the paper until you have the desired number of triangles to cut out. To simplify this step and to aid repetition you could make a paper bead template to draw around or if the paper is of a suitable size use a computer, a graphics package, and a printer to print the layout on to the paper.

Step 4. At this point it is worth noting that these measurements have been provided as a starting point, but ultimately it is the ratio of these measurements, combined with the overall length of the paper you are using plus the shapes that you use that will determine the dimensions and shape of your finished paper bead. Experiment!

Step 5. Carefully cut out the triangles using scissors or for a more accurate cut use a straight edge and a craft knife or rotary cutter.

Step 6. Take your skewer or dowel and starting at the wide end of your paper sample roll the paper around the skewer slightly so that it starts to form a cylinder. Once you are happy with the alignment roll this back and with a brush apply a little glue across the width of the paper immediately below the line of the skewer. Now carefully roll the paper past the glue and continue onwards ensuring that each spiral at the side of the bead is symmetrical as it forms. If you run out of alignment you can simply unroll the paper back as far as the last application of glue to correct the alignment.

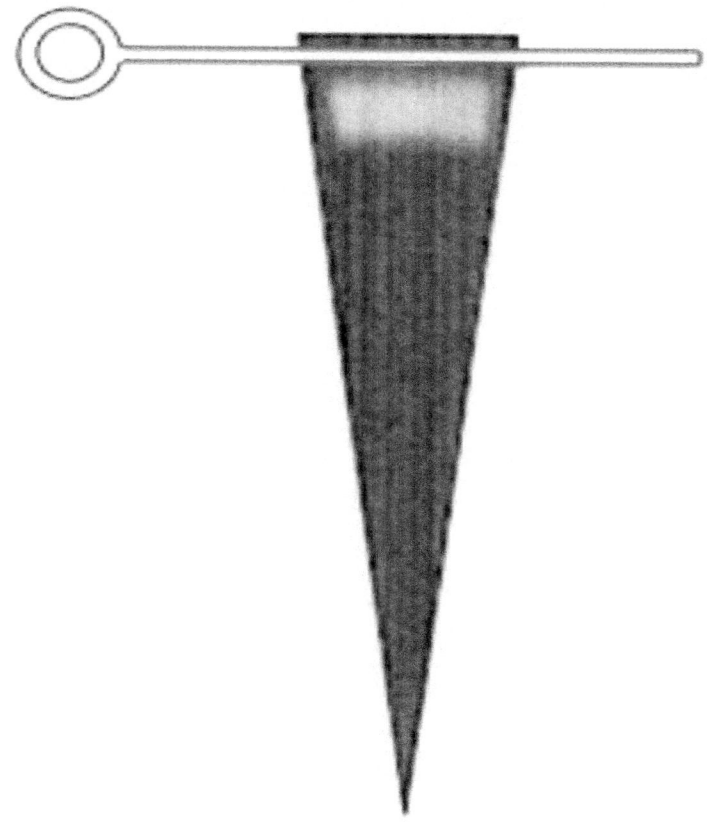

Step 7. At intervals apply another line of glue to secure your work so far. This is far cleaner than covering the whole triangle in glue at the outset.

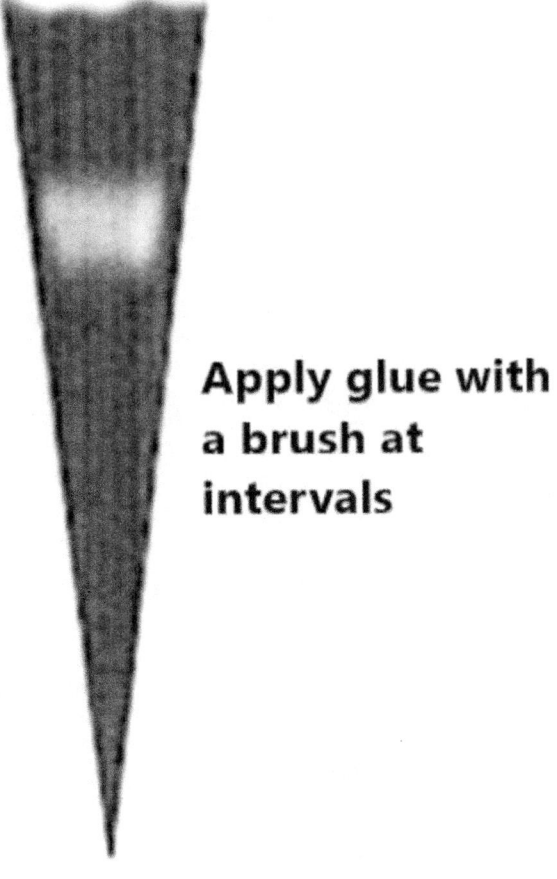

Apply glue with a brush at intervals

Step 8. When you have about 3 cm remaining, cover this remainder with a thin coat of glue leaving a border around the edges. When rolling the glue will be forced over this border without squeezing out over the sides of your beads.

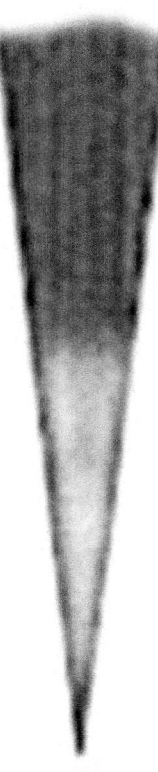

Apply glue with a brush to the final 3cm of the roll

Step 9. When the paper is completely rolled make sure the end is securely stuck down before rolling the bead through your fingers with a light pressure to ensure it is cylindrical and secure. If there is any glue residue at this point a quick gentle wipe with a damp cloth will suffice.

Step 10. Slide the hand rolled paper beads from the skewer or dowel and transfer it to a cocktail stick and set to one side in your florists block or polystyrene block to dry.

Step 11. When you have a good number of beads prepared you should then brush each bead with a few coats of varnish to make them water resistant. Follow the manufacturer's instructions, but ensure that when touch dry you rotate them on the cocktail stick so they don't stick when fully dry. Several thin coats over time give a much more polished result than one thick coat. Be patient for the best results!

Step 12. After you have finished your first run these instructions for making paper beads will be superfluous to requirements as it will all come naturally!

3. Refinements to this Paper Bead Making Technique:

Step 1. To make beads with different shapes, vary the size and shape of the paper triangles that you cut out. There are a number of different templates for making paper beads available on the internet. The following options are a guide but it is possible to add your own permutations:

Step 2. To provide a neater finish to your beads and to show more of the paper pattern, simply cut the tip from the triangle as indicated in the diagram above. This will give a broader end to the last part of the roll. This is particularly effective if you are using patterned paper or paper with text, as it will show the detail of the pattern or lettering.

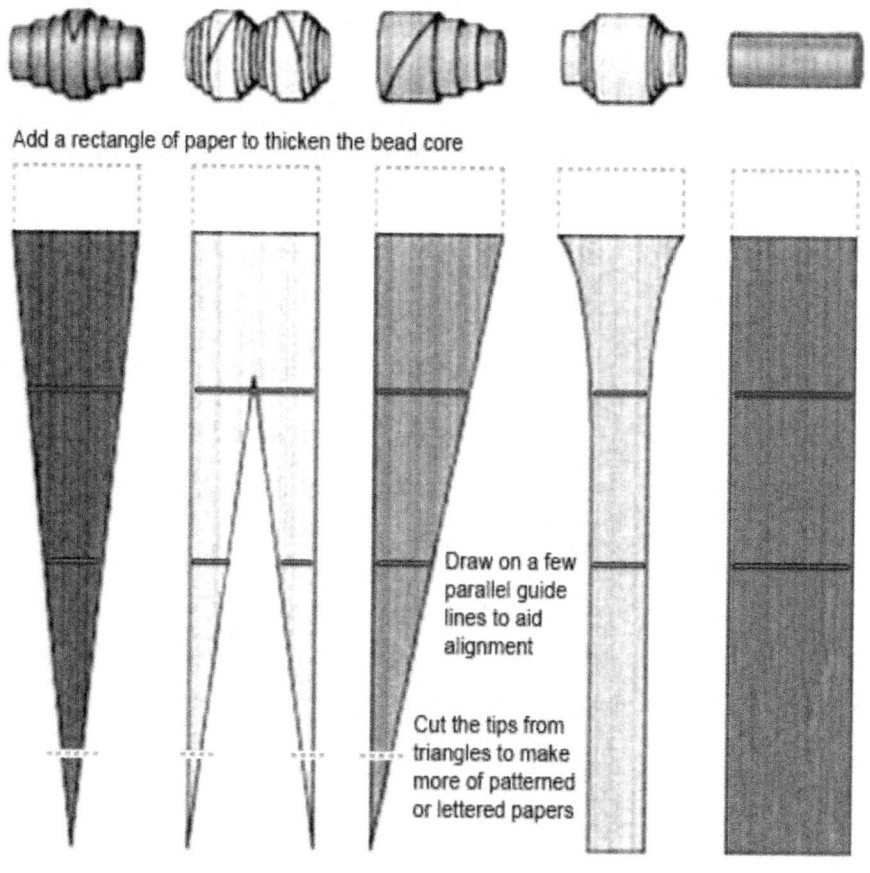

Add a rectangle of paper to thicken the bead core

Draw on a few parallel guide lines to aid alignment

Cut the tips from triangles to make more of patterned or lettered papers

Step 3. To provide a stronger, neater, flatter core to the finished paper bead add a rectangular area of paper to the long base of the triangle as shown in the diagram above. This doesn't need to be more than 1.5 cm long, and should simply allow for a few turns of the paper around the skewer or dowel. It also makes initial alignment of the paper easier. It has the added bonus of making the beads sit better against each other. On the downside, the initial stage of laying out the paper for cutting becomes more involved, but in the end it is worth the extra effort.

Step 4. To monitor progress and to ensure ongoing symmetry it is worthwhile adding some parallel pencilled lines to the back of the paper at the marking up stage.

Step 5. If you get bored with making straight edged beads invest in a guillotine or a pair of craft scissors with a decorative cutting edge – there are lots of patterns to choose from.

Step 6. Once you have a set of paper beads experiment with finishes and embellishments to add extra interest – be it gilding, wire wrapping, adding fancy papers, using specialist glazes, or simply painting them with acrylics, the options are endless.

Three Popular Type of Paper Beads

1. Round Paper Bead

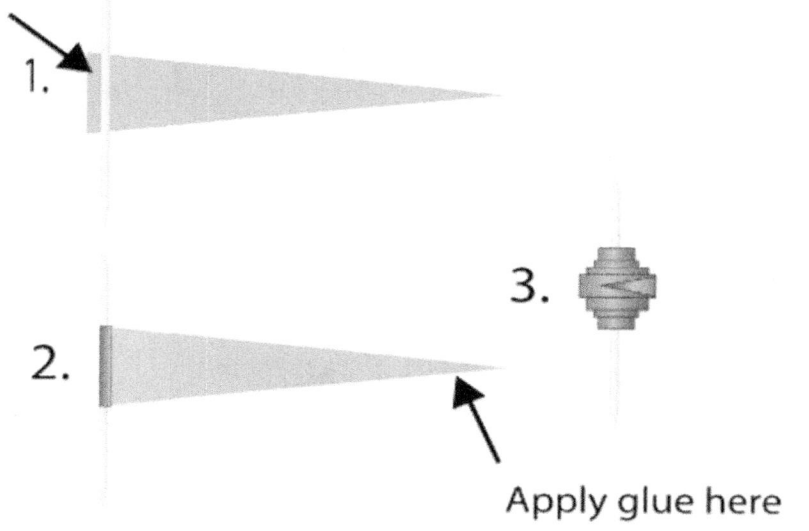

2. Tubular Paper Bead

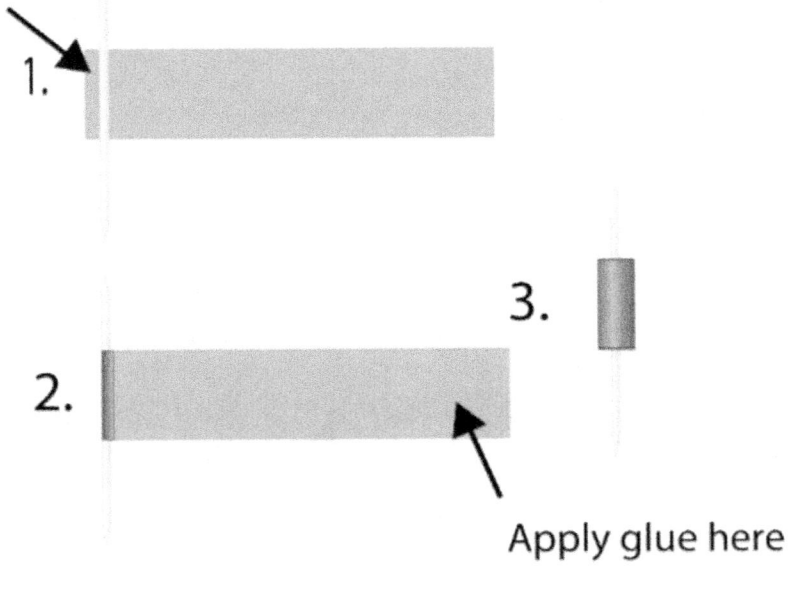

3. Teardrop Shaped Bead

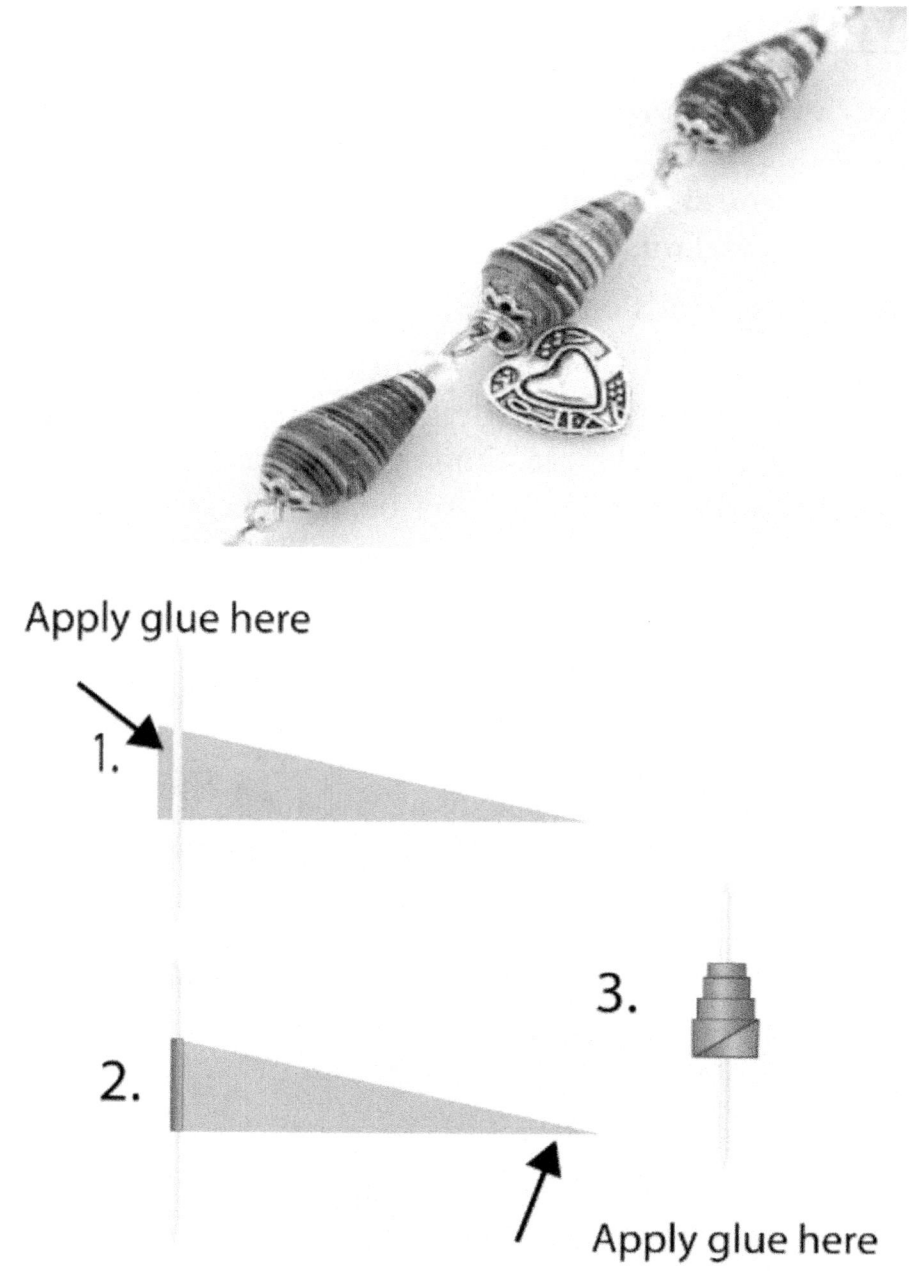

Sealing Paper Beads - Which Method Is Best?

Previous section described my new favorite tool for creating paper beads. The next step is to seal the beads with some kind of protective varnish. I tried 3 different sealants.

Method 1: ModPodge

The first thing I tried was painting each bead with 2 coats of ModPodge, mostly because it was just sitting there on my worktable. One of the trickiest parts was figuring out how to dry the beads. Thinking I was being clever, I stuck the pins in an old cardboard salt cylinder.

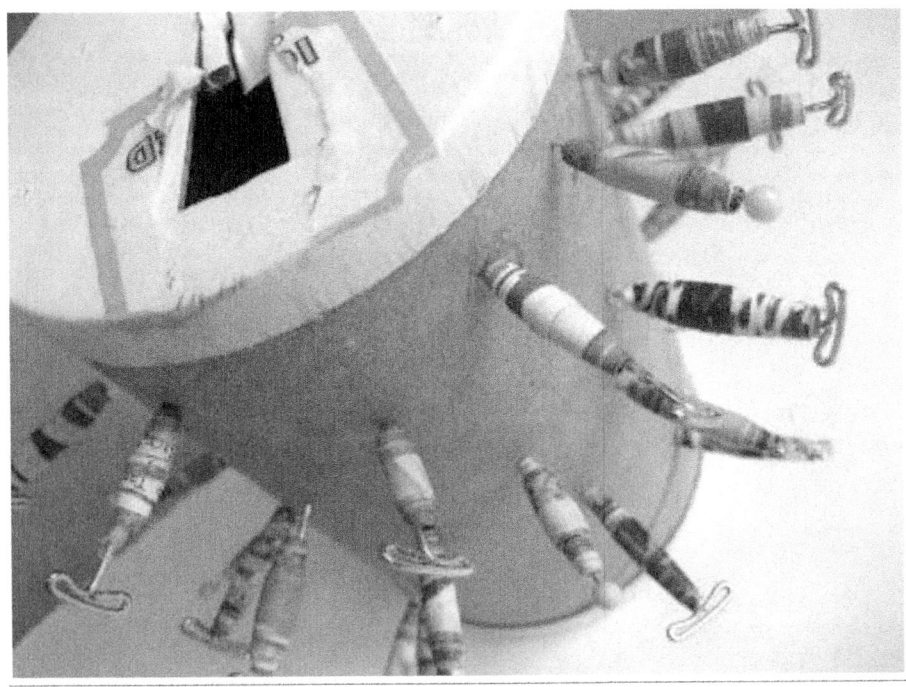

Sometimes what seems like a good upcycling idea isn't. The cardboard was too hard and pushing the pins in became a bloody mess. I switched to a foam block, which worked much better.

Pros

- Beads get covered evenly.
- Little danger of damaging the beads.
- You can sit at your worktable.

Cons

- It's time-consuming.
- The inside of the bead doesn't get coated.
- I'm not sure how well the ModPodge protects against water or wear-and-tear.

Method 2: Spray sealant

I found a can of clear fixative in my garage, and I thought I'd give it a try. I hung beads on a fishing line and went outside to spray them. Then I stood around for awhile, looking for a place to hang the sticky line. For round 2, I created a simple drying rack using bamboo skewers and a foam block. It made it much easier to both spray and dry the beads.

Pros

- It's fast.
- There's little chance of damage.

Cons

- It's hard to cover the beads evenly.
- The inside of the bead doesn't get covered.
- The varnish is flammable, so you have to go outside.
- You have to find a place to hang the beads.

Method 3: Varnish dip

For this method, I followed the detailed instructions written by Johnnie at Savedbylovecreations. I threaded the beads on fishing line with weights at the end, submerged them in water-based varnish, and hung them to dry.

This time, I figured out how to hang the drippy wet beads *before* I dipped them. I cobbled together this hanger out of bamboo skewers, pants hangers, and a wire stand. The contraption hangs in the outside stairwell in my backyard. It works fine, unless it rains, which it does often. Way too often.

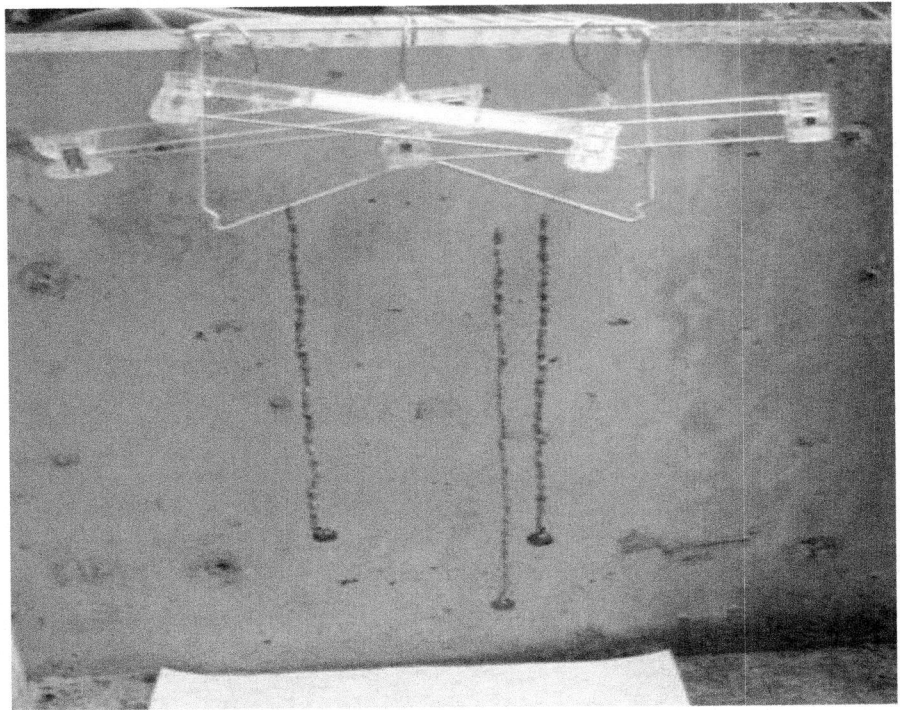

Pros

- Beads are covered evenly.
- Varnish covers both outside and inside of beads.
- If you dip the beads twice, they turn out very glossy (I used semi-gloss varnish here).

Cons

- This is the messiest method, but as long as you stick to water-based varnish, cleanup is easy.
- The beads stick together so ends can get damaged.
- The varnish is pricey (smaller cans are cheaper, but I don't think I could have fit the beads in).
- It takes several hours or more to dry, depending on the weather.
- This is subjective -- the varnish makes the beads feel processed, not natural, which is one of the things I like about paper beads -- they feel organic.

If you enjoyed the book, please leave a brief review on Amazon. I am very appreciative for your review as it truly make a difference. Thank you so much for purchasing this book and reading it to the end.

Printed in Great Britain
by Amazon